The Property Tax in North Carolina

Christopher B. McLaughlin

UNC | SCHOOL OF GOVERNMENT

About the Series

Local Government Board Builders offers local elected leaders practical advice on how to effectively lead and govern. The booklets in this series provide topic overviews, specific tips on effective practice, and worksheets and reflection questions to help local elected leaders improve their work. The series focuses on common activities for local governing boards, such as selecting and appointing committees and advisory boards, planning for the future, making better decisions, improving board accountability, and effectively engaging stakeholders in public decisions.

Vaughn Mamlin Upshaw, lecturer in public administration and government at the UNC School of Government, is the series editor.

Other Books in the Series

Leading Your Governing Board: A Guide for Mayors and County Board Chairs, Vaughn Mamlin Upshaw, 2009

A Model Code of Ethics for North Carolina Local Elected Officials, A. Fleming Bell, II, 2010

Creating and Maintaining Effective Local Government Citizen Advisory Committees, Vaughn Mamlin Upshaw, 2010

Working with Nonprofit Organizations, Margaret Henderson, Lydian Altman, Suzanne Julian, Gordon P. Whitaker, and Eileen R. Youens, 2010

Public Outreach and Participation, John B. Stephens, Ricardo S. Morse, and Kelley T. O'Brien, 2011

Local Government Revenue Sources in North Carolina, Kara A. Millonzi, 2011

Getting the Right Fit: The Governing Board's Role in Hiring a Manager, Vaughn Mamlin Upshaw, John A. Rible IV, and Carl W. Stenberg, 2011

Suggested Rules of Procedure for the Board of County Commissioners, Joseph S. Ferrell, Third Edition 2002

Suggested Rules of Procedure for Small Local Government Boards, A. Fleming Bell, II, Second Edition 1998

The School of Government at the University of North Carolina at Chapel Hill works to improve the lives of North Carolinians by engaging in practical scholarship that helps public officials and citizens understand and improve state and local government. Established in 1931 as the Institute of Government, the School provides educational, advisory, and research services for state and local governments. The School of Government is also home to a nationally ranked graduate program in public administration and specialized centers focused on information technology, environmental finance, and civic education for youth.

As the largest university-based local government training, advisory, and research organization in the United States, the School of Government offers up to 200 courses, seminars, and specialized conferences for more than 12,000 public officials each year. In addition, faculty members annually publish approximately fifty books, book chapters, bulletins, and other reference works related to state and local government. Each day that the General Assembly is in session, the School produces the *Daily Bulletin*, which reports on the day's activities for members of the legislature and others who need to follow the course of legislation.

The Master of Public Administration Program is a full-time, two-year program that serves up to sixty students annually. It consistently ranks among the best public administration graduate programs in the country, particularly in city management. With courses ranging from public policy analysis to ethics and management, the program educates leaders for local, state, and federal governments and nonprofit organizations.

Operating support for the School of Government's programs and activities comes from many sources, including state appropriations, local government membership dues, private contributions, publication sales, course fees, and service contracts. Visit www.sog.unc.edu or call 919.966.5381 for more information on the School's courses, publications, programs, and services.

Michael R. Smith, Dean
Thomas H. Thornburg, Senior Associate Dean
Frayda S. Bluestein, Associate Dean for Faculty Development
L. Ellen Bradley, Associate Dean for Programs and Marketing
Todd A. Nicolet, Associate Dean for Operations
Ann Cary Simpson, Associate Dean for Development
Bradley G. Volk, Associate Dean for Administration

FACULTY

Whitney Afonso	Joseph S. Ferrell	Janet Mason	Jessica Smith
Gregory S. Allison	Alyson A. Grine	Christopher B. McLaughlin	Karl W. Smith
David N. Ammons	Norma Houston	Laurie L. Mesibov	Carl W. Stenberg III
Ann M. Anderson	Cheryl Daniels Howell	Kara A. Millonzi	John B. Stephens
A. Fleming Bell, II	Jeffrey A. Hughes	Jill D. Moore	Charles Szypszak
Maureen M. Berner	Willow S. Jacobson	Jonathan Q. Morgan	Shannon H. Tufts
Mark F. Botts	Robert P. Joyce	Ricardo S. Morse	Vaughn Upshaw
Michael Crowell	Kenneth L. Joyner	C. Tyler Mulligan	Aimee N. Wall
Leisha DeHart-Davis	Diane M. Juffras	David W. Owens	Jeffrey B. Welty
Shea Riggsbee Denning	Dona G. Lewandowski	William C. Rivenbark	Richard B. Whisnant
James C. Drennan	Adam Lovelady	Dale J. Roenigk	
Richard D. Ducker	James M. Markham	John Rubin	

Contents

Introduction

The goal of this book is to educate local elected officials about their authority and obligations relating to the listing, assessment, levy, and collection of property taxes. After reading this book, members of local governing boards should know what they must do, what they may do, and, perhaps most importantly, what they cannot do with property taxes.

Property taxes are only one of the many revenue sources available to local governments. Readers seeking to better understand the full range of these revenues are encouraged to read the Local Government Board Builders book *Local Government Revenue Sources in North Carolina,* authored by my School of Government colleague Kara Millonzi.

Non-Legal Considerations

This book focuses mainly on the legal issues surrounding property taxes. But local government elected officials also face a number of important non-legal decisions concerning property tax policy and practice.

The most basic of these decisions is whether the local government wishes to levy a property tax. Although property taxes are optional, all 100 counties and nearly all of the state's 500-plus municipalities levy this type of tax.

Taxpayers may wonder why local governments tax at all, in light of the substantial federal and state taxes already affecting their incomes and activities. The simple answer to this question is that without property tax revenues, local governments would be forced to drastically cut their services. Property taxes are the single largest source of unrestricted revenues for both counties and municipalities in North Carolina. Revenue from the taxes supports the wide variety of services provided by local governments.

The property tax is popular among local governments because it is one of the few revenue sources that is under their complete control. Most other taxes are levied at rates set by state statutes or produce revenue that must be shared with the state or with other local governments. Not so for property tax rates and revenues, which are controlled entirely by local governments and subject only to a rather generous statutory maximum rate.

Property tax rates vary across the state from just a few pennies to over one dollar per $100 of property value. The legal parameters concerning the tax rate calculation are discussed under "The Property Tax Rate," below. But for the most part, the tax rate decision will rest on a policy question beyond the scope of this book: What level of services should the local government provide and how should those services be funded?

Other non-legal decisions include how to organize the tax office, whether a municipality should collect its own taxes or contract with the county for such services, what types of enforced collection actions the collector will be authorized to pursue and when countywide reappraisals of real property should occur. This book discusses the relevant statutory constraints and identifies best practices, but it does not attempt to suggest the correct answers to these questions. As with most local government issues, there is no one-size-fits-all approach to property taxes.

Questions for Discussion

1. Does your local government levy a property tax? If so, what is the current rate?

2. When was your county's last general tax reappraisal of real property? When is the next one scheduled?

The Big Picture

Property taxes represent the single largest source of unrestricted revenue for both counties and municipalities. For fiscal year 2010–2011, property taxes represented 52 percent of county revenues and nearly 25 percent of municipal revenues. Figures 1 and 2 illustrate the relative importance of property taxes as compared to other revenue sources. Note that both figures exclude debt proceeds, which must be paid back in the future using other revenue sources and are therefore not truly revenue sources themselves.

Although utility fees represent a larger percentage of municipal revenues than do property taxes, those funds are not *unrestricted* revenues because they generally must be used to cover the cost of providing those utilities. If utility fees and charges were excluded from the calculation, property taxes would represent more than 37 percent of municipal revenues.

In recent years North Carolina local governments' reliance on property taxes has grown as other revenue sources have suffered. Consider the sales tax: economic woes since the Great Recession of 2008, combined with the loss of a portion of counties' local sales tax authority as part of the 2007 state Medicaid funding reform legislation, have reduced

Figure 1.   2010–11 County Revenues (\$11.18 Billion total excluding debt)

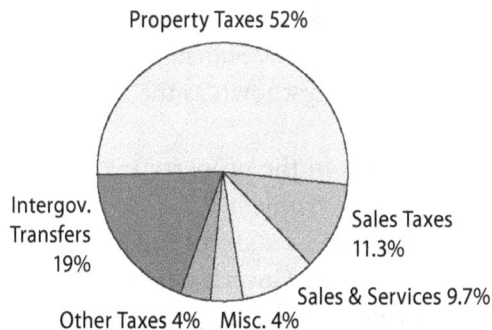

Property Taxes 52%
Intergov. Transfers 19%
Sales Taxes 11.3%
Sales & Services 9.7%
Other Taxes 4%   Misc. 4%

Source: N.C. Department of State Treasurer

Figure 2.   2010–11 Municipal Revenues (\$9.25 Billion total excluding debt)

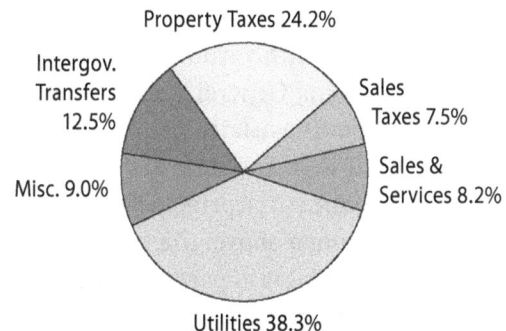

Property Taxes 24.2%
Intergov. Transfers 12.5%
Sales Taxes 7.5%
Sales & Services 8.2%
Misc. 9.0%
Utilities 38.3%

Source: N.C. Department of State Treasurer

Figure 3.   Combined County and Municipal Sales and Use Tax Revenues Compared to Combined County and Municipal Property Tax Revenues ($ Billions)

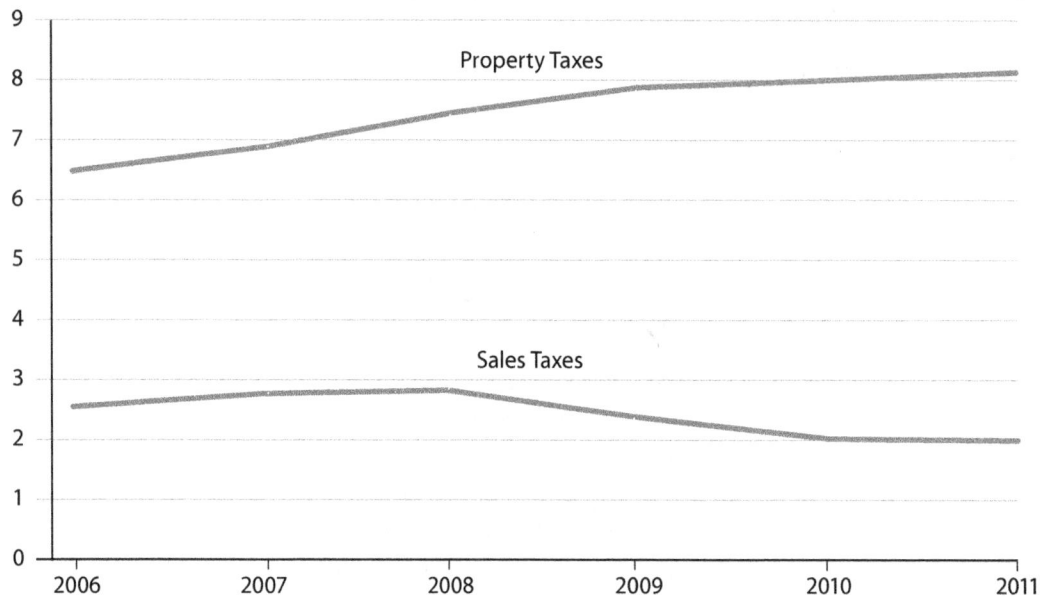

Source: N.C. Department of State Treasurer

county sales and use tax revenues by more than one-third since their peak in fiscal year 2007–2008. As Figure 3 illustrates, property tax revenues have remained far more stable during the same period.

The Governing Law and the Cast of Characters

The North Carolina Constitution, Article V (Finance), Section 2 (State and local taxation), sets the basic ground rules for property taxes. Chapter 105, Subchapter II, of the North Carolina General Statutes (hereinafter G.S.), commonly known as the Machinery Act, provides the details.

Actors at both the state and local levels play major roles in the property tax process. Table 1 identifies the principal characters at both levels of government.

As mentioned above, the property tax process is governed by statutes enacted by the **General Assembly** as part of the Machinery Act. The state **Local Government Division of the N.C. Department of Revenue** is charged with ensuring that local governments adhere to the Machinery Act's requirements. This division also provides education, training, and

Table 1.   Property Tax Cast of Characters

State Level	Local Level
General Assembly	Governing Board
Department of Revenue, Local Government Division	Assessor (County)
Property Tax Commission	Tax Collector
Court of Appeals	Board of Equalization and Review (County)
Supreme Court	

guidance to local government tax officials and assesses and allocates public service company property to the counties so that it can be subject to local property taxes.

Note that the Department of Revenue's Local Government Division is distinct from the Local Government Commission (LGC), which operates out of the N.C. Department of the State Treasurer. The LGC monitors the fiscal and accounting practices of the state's local governments, but does not play a direct role in property tax administration.

County **boards of equalization and review**, the state **Property Tax Commission,** the state **court of appeals,** and the state **supreme court** are all involved with the resolution of appeals concerning property tax values and property tax exemptions and exclusions.

The **assessor** is responsible for listing and assessing all taxable property in the county for property taxes. In other words, he or she must determine the what, the where, the who, and the how much for all property that will be taxed for the coming fiscal year. The **tax collector** must collect the taxes levied on that property, if necessary by use of the enforced collection remedies available under the Machinery Act and other statutes. In

---

Why is it called the "Machinery Act" and where can I find it?

G.S. 105-271 and -272 state that the collection of property tax statutes in Subchapter II of Chapter 105 can be referred to as the Machinery Act because "[t]he purpose of this Subchapter is to provide the *machinery* for the listing, appraisal, and assessment of property and the levy and collection of taxes on property by counties and municipalities." (emphasis added)

   The North Carolina Department of Revenue usually produces a hard copy of the Machinery Act every two years to capture the most recent changes to its many sections. The most recent version is dated 2011 and reflects legislation enacted during the 2011 legislative session. However, because the Machinery Act is amended almost every legislative session and the hard copy is produced only every other year, the best source for the most up-to-date Machinery Act provisions is the searchable General Statutes page on the General Assembly's website, www.ncga.state.nc.us/gascripts/statutes/Statutes.asp.

Table 2.　Rights and Duties of Local Government Governing Boards

Board of County Commissioners

Adopts property tax rate annually

Appoints assessor and tax collector

Reviews performance of assessor and tax collector

Accepts settlement of prior year's taxes from tax collector and charges tax collector with responsibility for current year's taxes

Decides when to conduct countywide reappraisals of real property (at least every eight years)

Appoints Board of Equalization and Review (the county commissioners may serve as this board)

Rules on taxpayer requests for refunds and releases

Town/City Council

Adopts property tax rate annually

Appoints tax collector *or* contracts with county for tax collection

Reviews performance of tax collector

Accepts settlement of prior year's taxes from tax collector and charges tax collector with responsibility for current year's taxes

Rules on taxpayer requests for refunds and releases

Table 3.　Important Dates on the Property Tax Calendar

January 1

Listing date (ownership, situs, value, and taxability determined)

Tax liens attach to real property

July 1

Fiscal year begins

Deadline for adoption of new budget and tax rate

September 1

Discounts end (if offered)

Taxes due

January 6 (following year)

Taxes become delinquent, interest accrues, and enforced collections may begin

June 30 (following year)

Fiscal year ends, annual collection rate is determined

many counties, the commissioners have chosen to appoint a single individual as both assessor and tax collector under the title of "tax administrator."

The role of the **local government governing board** in the property tax process is summarized in Table 2. Table 3 lists the important dates in the property tax calendar. More details on all of these issues are provided in subsequent chapters.

Real Property versus Personal Property

Collection remedies under the Machinery Act differ depending on whether the property being taxed is real or personal. Real property is essentially land, buildings, and things that are permanently affixed to those buildings—think of light fixtures or kitchen cabinets.

Personal property is everything else: vehicles, boats, planes, business equipment, and so forth. With very few exceptions, personal property is taxable only if it is tangible. Intangible personal property—such as cash, stocks, bank deposits, patents, and franchise rights—is not taxable.

Why Cars Are Different

Cars, trucks, vans, motorcycles, and trailers with valid registrations and license plates are called "registered motor vehicles" (RMVs) by the Machinery Act. Although they are considered personal property under the Machinery Act, RMVs are subject to very different tax rules than those applied to other types of personal property.

In a nutshell, the taxation of RMVs is tied to the registration and renewal process. Registration of most motor vehicles is staggered throughout the year, so that different due dates and delinquency dates exist for different RMV taxpayers.

Since 1993 the process has worked like this: when a taxpayer registers a motor vehicle, the N.C. Division of Motor Vehicles (DMV) sends notice of that registration to the assessor for the county in which the motor vehicle is registered. The assessor then assigns a value to that motor vehicle and sends a tax bill to the owner. If the tax bill is not paid, the tax collector could ask the DMV to block a renewal of the motor vehicle's registration. But that remedy would not affect the owner until the current registration expired months later. And many owners would simply fail to renew their registrations and risk driving unregistered vehicles rather than paying the taxes.

Tax collection percentages on registered motor vehicles tend to lag well behind those for other property taxes, due to both the mobility of the vehicles and the special tax rules that apply to them. In an effort to improve RMV collections, the General Assembly adopted new taxation rules that (as of this publication) are to take effect in July 2013. Under the new system, taxes on RMVs will be collected by the DMV at the time of initial registration or renewal of an existing registration. If the owner refuses to pay the taxes, the DMV will refuse to register the motor vehicle. Massive changes in tax software and business practices will be required to implement the new system, but the expectation is that once it is up and running, collection rates on RMV taxes will rise closer to the level of those for other property taxes. See "Registered Motor Vehicles," below, for more details on RMV taxes.

Questions for Discussion

1. How much revenue did your local government's property tax generate last fiscal year? What percentage of your local government's total revenues did property tax revenues represent?

2. For counties, when was the assessor first appointed? When does the assessor's current term end? When was the tax collector first appointed? When does the tax collector's term end? Does the same person serve as both assessor and tax collector?

3. For municipalities, does the municipality collect its own property tax or does it contract with the county for this service?

   a. If the county collects the municipality's taxes, how is the county's compensation calculated?

   b. If the municipality collects its own taxes, when was the tax collector first appointed? When does the tax collector's term end?

The Property Tax Rate

Although local governments are not required to levy property taxes, nearly all do. The rates at which they levy those taxes vary greatly, as Table 4 indicates.

Traditionally the lowest county rates were found along the coast and in the mountains in counties with lots of expensive vacation homes. But the national real estate slump has hit the North Carolina vacation home market harder than the primary home market. Some counties with lots of vacation homes are experiencing dramatic drops in their real property tax bases and as a result have been forced to raise their tax rates substantially. Carteret County, for example, raised its tax rate more than 30 percent following its 2011 reappraisal, due to the unprecedented decrease in its real property tax base.

Property tax rates for a particular local government are generally capped at $1.50, but that cap is subject to many exceptions. For example, there is no statutory limit on the rate for property taxes that are used to fund schools or jails (see below for a discussion of use-specific property taxes). And for uses that are subject to the statutory cap, a local government may obtain voter approval to exceed the $1.50 maximum tax rate.

As Table 4 demonstrates, no local government comes even close to the $1.50 maximum tax rate. This "tax gap"—the difference between actual property tax rates and the statutory maximum for those rates—is often a point of contention when local governments seeks additional revenue from the General Assembly. From the state legislature's perspective, local governments have ample opportunity to generate more revenue from local property taxes and therefore do not need additional revenue from state coffers. Local governments obviously have a different perspective on this issue.

How do I use the tax rate to calculate a tax bill?

Tax rates are expressed as "$ of tax per $100 dollars of taxable value." For example, if a home is valued for tax purposes at $200,000 and the county tax rate is $.25, the county property taxes on that home will be $500. First divide the taxable value by 100 ($200,000/100 = $2,000), then multiply the result by the tax rate ($2,000 x .25 = $500).

Table 4. County and Municipal Property Tax Rates (2011–2012)

	Lowest Rate	Highest Rate	Average Rate
Counties	.279 (Macon)	.99 (Scotland)	.64
Municipalities	.0165 (Wesley Chapel)	.82 (Roper)	.43

Source: N.C. Department of Revenue, www.dor.state.nc.us/publications/propertyrates.html

The $1.50 cap applies to individual taxing jurisdictions, not to individual taxpayers. A taxpayer who lives in a municipality could very well wind up paying a total property tax rate of greater than $1.50, because that taxpayer's property is subject to both county and municipal taxes. As a result, a municipality need not worry about the county's property tax when setting its own rate, or vice versa.

Tax Rate Uniformity and Tax Districts

Article V, Section 2, of the North Carolina Constitution requires that all property within a specific taxing jurisdiction must be subject to the same tax rate. This uniformity requirement prohibits local governments from adopting different tax rates for different property or for different areas of that jurisdiction. For example, a county could not adopt one tax rate for real property and a different tax rate for motor vehicles. Nor could a county choose to adopt one tax rate for its incorporated areas and a different tax rate for its unincorporated areas.

The only exception to the uniformity requirement is the constitutional provision that permits special tax districts. Often called service districts, these tax districts are authorized by Article V, Section 2(4), of the North Carolina Constitution to fund additional services in their geographic areas. Multiple tax districts are permitted in the same local government, so long as each tax district is created for a permissible purpose.

Counties most often use special tax districts to fund fire protection in unincorporated areas, but they can also use them to fund services such as trash collection, sewer and water systems, and beach erosion control. Cities can use municipal tax districts to fund many of those same services, but they more often create districts for downtown revitalization projects. This category is broadly defined to cover a variety of expenditures including new parking facilities, improved lighting, additional police protection, and tourism promotion within the downtown city core.

Another type of special tax district is a special supplemental school district. The supplemental school district tax must be approved by voters before it can be levied and must be used only to fund the public schools in that district. Once adopted, a supplemental school tax applies to all property within that particular school district.

The taxes levied in a special tax district count toward the $1.50 cap on general property tax rates. This means that the total of regular property taxes and special district taxes levied by a local government on a particular piece of property cannot exceed $1.50 for certain uses unless the local government obtains voter approval to exceed that cap.

Use-Specific Taxes

A local government may adopt a single property tax rate to satisfy all of its budgetary needs, or it may adopt multiple tax rates with the revenue from each earmarked for a specific use. For example, instead of funding police and fire protection services out of its general property tax revenue, a city could choose to adopt two property tax rates: one for general fund revenue and one to fund police and fire services.

There is no limit on the number of different use-specific property tax rates that may be adopted, so long as each such tax applies uniformly to all taxable property within the jurisdiction. Use-specific taxes may be adopted as part of the local government's annual budget and do not require voter approval.

A key difference between use-specific property taxes and special tax district taxes is that use-specific taxes must apply to the entire jurisdiction. Special tax district taxes may be levied on portions of a jurisdiction to fund specific services in that district.

The North Carolina Supreme Court has ruled that local governments' spending decisions are not bound by use-specific property taxes. A local government may change its spending for a particular use regardless of what it promised to spend on that use in its budget through a use-specific tax rate.

For example, assume that a county adopts a $.50 general tax rate, a $.12 tax rate for law enforcement, and a $.02 tax rate for libraries. Based on its budgeted tax base, the $.12 tax would raise $1,200,000 for county law enforcement and the $.02 tax would raise $200,000 for county libraries. Despite the adoption of the use-specific taxes, the county could choose to spend more or less than these amounts on law enforcement and libraries in the coming fiscal year. Voters may not take kindly to such variations from the budget, but they are legal.

Calculating the Tax Rate

Assume Carolina County needs to generate $50,000,000 in property tax revenue to balance its budget for the coming fiscal year. The basic property tax calculation is as follows:

$$(Tax\ Base / 100) \times Tax\ Rate = Tax\ Revenue$$

First, the county should get from the tax collector the estimated property tax collection percentage for the current fiscal year. This percentage will be an estimate because the current fiscal year will not have ended at the time Carolina County creates the budget for the next fiscal year.

Assume the estimated collection percentage for the current fiscal year is 97 percent. The county should divide the revenue target by this percentage to account for the fact that not every penny of the property tax levy will be collected.

$$\$50,000,000 / .97 = \$51,550,000$$

The result is the adjusted revenue target for the next fiscal year. In other words, if the county wishes to produce $50,000,000 in property tax revenue next year, it must levy $51,550,000 in property taxes.

Second, the county should get from the assessor the estimated tax base for the next fiscal year. It will be an estimate because subsequent tax appeals, discoveries, and motor vehicle registrations will affect the final figure.

Assume that the estimated tax base is $10,000,000,000. The county should divide the estimated tax base by 100, to reflect the fact that the tax rate is "per $100 in value."

$$\$10,000,000,000 / \$100 = \$100,000,000$$

Finally, the county should divide the adjusted revenue target by the result above to determine the rate.

$$\$51,550,000 / \$100,000,000 = \$.516$$

Carolina County must levy a property tax of $.516, or 51.6 cents per $100 of value, to meet its budgetary needs for the coming fiscal year.

When budgeting, many local governments start with a tax rate target rather than a revenue target. Regardless of the approach used, the local government must account for the current year's tax collection percentage when budgeting for next year.

For example, assume that Carolina County wishes to keep its tax rate at $.51 per $100 of value for the coming year. If next year's tax base is estimated to be $10,000,000,000, a tax rate of $.51 would produce tax revenue of $51,000,000. However, this estimated revenue must be reduced by this year's collection percentage:

$$\$51,000,000 \times .97 = \$49,470,000$$

As a result, if Carolina County plans to keep its tax rate at $.51 for the coming year, it should budget for no more than $49,470,000 in property tax revenue.

Setting the Tax Rate

Property taxes are levied on a fiscal year basis, despite the fact that many of the important dates on the property tax schedule seem to be configured around the calendar year. A local government that levies property taxes must set its property tax rate(s) in its annual budget, which should be adopted by July 1, the beginning of the fiscal year.

Until a budget is adopted, there can be no property tax levy. Although interim budgets are permitted, they authorize only continued spending by local governments and not the levy of taxes. A delay in the adoption of the budget can delay property tax collections and do serious harm to a local government's revenues.

The property tax rate should be based on the amount of revenue the local government needs to balance its budget after all other revenue sources are accounted for, given the expected tax base for the coming year. Obviously this amount will be driven by important decisions regarding what services the local government can and should provide.

When balancing the budget with property taxes, a local government must be realistic about how much of its tax levy it will actually collect. While property tax collection percentages are generally very good—over 97 percent on average—no local government collects every penny of its property taxes. For budget purposes, state law prohibits local governments from assuming a higher collection rate for the coming year than it experienced in the current year.

Changing the Tax Rate

Once the total tax rate is set in the budget, the governing board is generally prohibited from changing it. Absent an order from a judge or from the Local Government Commission, the only justification for adjusting a tax rate after adoption of the budget is when the local government receives revenues that are substantially different than expected. And even then the change must occur before January 1 following the start of the fiscal year. For example, if a governing wished to change its 2013–2014 tax rate due to a substantial change in revenues, it would need to act before January 1, 2014.

What type of events could justify a change in the total tax rate under this standard? The relevant statutes do not provide additional details, but presumably changes could occur after a misfortune such as a bankruptcy filing by a large industrial taxpayer that would prevent collection of a substantial portion of the local government's property tax levy or the elimination of an important revenue source due to new legislation enacted by the General Assembly. Good news—such as the creation of a major new revenue source for the local government—could also justify a mid-year change in the tax rate, but sadly, such occurrences seem quite rare.

As mentioned above, local governments may adopt multiple tax rates for different uses. These use-specific rates may be changed during a fiscal year without regard for statutory restrictions so long as the total tax rate levied by the local government does not change.

Consider again the example in which a county adopts a general tax rate of $.50, a law enforcement tax of $.12, and a library tax of $.02, for a total combined rate of $.64. The county would be free to alter any or all of its three different tax rates so long as the total combined rate still equaled $.64.

The Revenue-Neutral Tax Rate

To help taxpayers compare tax rates before and after countywide reappraisals of real property, local governments are required to calculate and publish revenue-neutral tax rates (RNTRs) following their reappraisals.

The RNTR is the tax rate that would produce the same amount of revenue using the new tax base as was produced in the present year from the existing tax rate and tax base. If the new tax rate adopted by the governing board is higher than the RNTR, then the local government has increased its total property tax levy. If the new rate is lower than the RNTR, then the local government has decreased its total property tax levy.

In normal economic times, tax bases increase after reappraisals. When the tax base increases, the tax rate can be lowered without decreasing tax revenue. As a result, the RNTR is normally lower than the existing tax rate.

But when market prices are dropping as they have in many areas of the state recently, a local government's tax base can decrease after a reappraisal. In these circumstances, if the government board wishes to keep revenues constant it must raise the tax rate. As a result, the RNTR will be higher than the existing tax rate.

Local governments are not required to adopt the RNTR, but they must publish it as part of their annual budget process. Even if the RNTR is adopted, individual taxpayers may see their tax bills increase or decrease because their individual property appreciated or depreciated more than did the tax base in the aggregate. Much confusion surrounds the RNTR, in large part because, despite its name, it does not guarantee that taxpayers' bills will remain constant.

For example, assume that Carolina County's tax base increased by 10 percent following its 2013 reappraisal. The RNTR is calculated to be $.50 per $100 of value, a bit lower than the county's 2012–2013 tax rate of $.55 per $100 of value. The county commissioners decide to adopt the RNTR as the tax rate for 2013–2014 and proudly announce that they have avoided a tax increase. However, when the 2013–2014 tax bills are mailed in August, Tommy TarHeel is furious because his new tax bill is higher than last year's tax bill.

How can this be? The likely answer is that Tommy's real property appreciated more than 10 percent, which was the average increase in value for all real property in the county. Assume that Tommy's real property tax appraisal increased from $100,000 to $150,000 as a result of the 2013 reappraisal. For 2012–2013, Tommy's tax bill was $550 ($100,000/100 × $.55). For 2013–2014, his tax bill is $750 ($150,000/100 x $.50). The drop in the tax rate was not enough to offset the increase in Tommy's tax appraisal, meaning that Tommy's tax bill increased $200 despite the county's adoption of the RNTR.

By adopting the RNTR, a local government may keep its aggregate property tax revenue constant. But individual taxpayers' bills are not guaranteed to remain constant because individual properties are likely to have appreciated or depreciated differently than did the countywide tax base.

Questions for Discussion

1. What is your local government's property tax rate? Has that rate changed over the past few years?

2. Has your local government created any special tax districts? If so, what are the tax rates in those districts and for what purposes are those tax revenues used? Are there other public needs that could be funded through special tax districts?

3. What was your local government's most recent revenue-neutral tax rate? How did that compare with the then-existing tax rate? Was it adopted for the following tax year?

Listing and Assessing

The process of determining what taxable property exists in a jurisdiction, who owns it, and how much it is worth is known as listing and assessing property for taxation. The county assessor oversees this process, which is closely regulated by the Machinery Act and is intended to be (mostly) uniform from county to county. The only property over which the assessor does not have listing and assessing authority is public service company property, described in more detail below.

As a general rule, local government governing boards do not get involved with assigning tax values to individual properties. That process is accomplished by the assessor and his or her staff, ideally free from political pressures.

However, local government governing boards—especially boards of county commissioners—do retain some discretion as to how and when the process unfolds. These discretionary duties include

- appointing the assessor and setting his/her term of office;
- approving the budget for the assessor's office;
- deciding when to hold countywide reappraisals of real property;
- ruling on taxpayer appeals of tax values and tax exemptions while sitting as the board of equalization and review (or appointing a separate board of equalization and review); and
- waiving or refusing to waive discovery bills.

One property tax issue over which local governments have no authority is the creation of property tax exemptions. The North Carolina Constitution grants this authority exclusively to the General Assembly. As a result, property tax exemptions are products of state statutes, not local ordinances. Counties and municipalities may not create their own exemptions from property taxes. Nor may they decide to ignore exemptions mandated by the Machinery Act.

This chapter briefly describes the listing and assessing process and the appropriate role for governing boards in that process. Readers who seek more details should take a look at *A Guide to the Listing, Assessment, and Taxation of Property in North Carolina*, a comprehensive guide to the process written by my School of Government colleague Shea Denning.

Appointing the Assessor

The assessor is appointed by the board of county commissioners and is charged with responsibility for listing and assessing all taxable property in the county. This process includes determining the situs—a fancy word for taxable location—of that property, determining who owns that property, deciding whether that property and its owner are eligible for an exemption or exclusion from tax, and, perhaps most controversially, assigning a value for tax purposes to that property.

The Machinery Act creates some minimum qualifications for assessors, but for the most part the board of county commissioner retains great discretion as to who should serve in this role. Candidates must be at least twenty-one years of age, must hold a high school diploma or equivalent, and must be certified by the N.C. Department of Revenue within two years of taking office. Certification involves passing four assessment courses and a comprehensive exam. The assessor must be appointed for a fixed term set by the county commissioners that can vary in length from two to four years. Once the assessor's term length is set by the commissioners, it cannot be changed until after the term ends or after the assessor is removed from office.

Why are there no municipal assessors?

More than five hundred North Carolina cities and towns levy property taxes, but not a single one lists and assesses its own property for tax purposes. The Machinery Act requires municipalities to rely on the county assessor to answer the what, where, who, and how much questions relating to property taxes, with one exception. Any municipality that sits in more than one county is authorized to appoint its own assessor to list and assess all of its property for taxation. Plenty of cities and towns qualify for this exception, but none takes advantage of it. The reasons behind those decisions likely vary from town to town, but the expense involved is almost certainly a driving factor. Why pay for a service that the municipality can get for free from the county? Taxpayer confusion may be another consideration. If a municipality were to appoint its own assessor, taxpayers residing in that jurisdiction could wind up with two different tax values placed on their homes, cars, and other taxable property—one assigned by the county and one assigned by the municipality. More than a few taxpayers would question this result.

Unlike most employees in most counties, assessors are not at-will employees and cannot be removed from office at the discretion of the commissioners. An assessor may be removed from office before his or her term ends only for "good cause," a term not defined by the Machinery Act. However, similar good cause provisions covering appointed officials elsewhere in the General Statutes suggest that adequate grounds for removal include inefficiency, misconduct in office, and commission of a felony or other crime involving moral turpitude. In other words, the conduct that justifies the removal must either be directly tied to the assessor's job performance or be so serious as to call into question the assessor's fitness for office. For example, the failure to pay property taxes in a timely fashion likely would justify the firing of an assessor, but a conviction for driving under the influence might not.

If the county commissioners wish to remove the assessor from office, they must first provide the assessor written notice of that intent and the opportunity be heard at a public session of the board. For obvious reasons, the county attorney should be intimately involved with this process.

The Machinery Act does not create term limits for assessors. A board can repeatedly reappoint a particular assessor for as long as it wishes.

What, Where, Who, and How Much?

The what, where, who, and how much decisions concerning property taxes on *personal* property are made as of the annual listing day, which is the January 1 before the fiscal year begins. For taxes on *real* property, the how much decisions (appraisals) are made as of January 1 of the reappraisal year, but the ownership and taxability decisions are made as of January 1 each year just as they are for personal property. In other words, a snapshot is taken every January 1, and the results of that snapshot control property taxes for the coming fiscal year.

For example, if Tom Taxpayer buys a new boat on February 1, 2012, he will not be required to list that boat for 2012–2013 property taxes because he did not own the boat on January 1. If Tina Taxpayer owns a house in Carolina County on January 1, 2012, that house is taxable by the county for the 2012–2013 fiscal year even if it burns to the ground the very next day. If Tim Taxpayer owns a vacant lot in Carolina County on January 1, 2012, and breaks ground on a new house on that lot on January 2, the new house will not be taxable by the county for 2012–2013 because it did not exist on January 1, the listing day. The house first will be listed and taxed as of January 1, *2013*, meaning it first will be taxed by the county in the 2013–2014 fiscal year.

Situs

The situs (taxable location) of real property should be easily determined and immutable except when cities change their boundaries through annexation or de-annexation or, more rarely, when two counties adjust their borders. But the situs of personal property—cars, boats, and planes especially—can present a major challenge. The fact that movable property is not in a jurisdiction on January 1 does not necessarily mean that the jurisdiction cannot tax that property for the coming year.

With respect to personal property, situs means property that is more or less permanently located in a jurisdiction. For example, if a private jet is flown all over the country throughout the year but always returns to a hangar in Carolina County, Carolina County should be able to tax that plane even if it is not in the county on January 1.

Appraisal of Personal Property

The Machinery Act requires that all property be assessed for tax purposes at its "true value," defined to be the property's market value were it sold in an arms-length transaction between two willing, able, and informed parties under no compulsion to buy or sell the property.

As mentioned above, all taxable personal property—in other words, all taxable property that is not land or buildings—is appraised annually as of January 1. Generally tax appraisals for cars, boats, planes, factory equipment, and other personal property decrease from year to year because that property depreciates and loses value over time.

Appraisal of Real Property

The most time-consuming and controversial part of the property tax process is the county-wide reappraisal of real property, during which all land and buildings are assigned new tax values. Just as is true for personal property, real property must be valued at its true market value that would be obtained in an arms-length transaction. Because foreclosure sales are involuntary sales, they are generally not considered when calculating appraisals.

Reappraisals, or "revals" as they are commonly called, must occur at least every eight years. Within this eight-year limitation, a county can choose whatever reappraisal cycle it prefers. A county is also free to change its reappraisal cycle in between reappraisals, so long as it stays within the eight-year limitation.

**Figure 4.   Reappraisal Cycles across N.C. Counties
(as reported to N.C. Department of Revenue for 2011)**

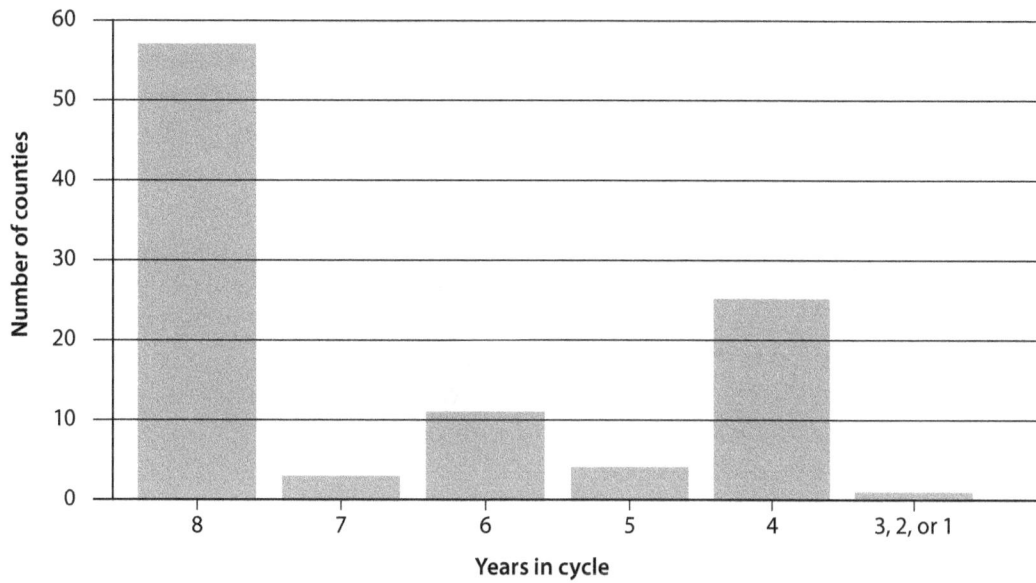

Source: N.C. Department of State Treasurer

In an ideal world, every county would reappraise all of its real property every year so that its tax values would be pegged to true market value as closely as possible. But annual reappraisal of the many thousands of real estate parcels in each county is simply not practical from either an expense or a workload perspective. As Figure 4 demonstrates, just over half of the state's 100 counties are on eight-year cycles and about one-quarter of them are on four-year cycles. No county regularly conducts reappraisals more frequently than every four years.

Depending on the size of its assessor's office, a county can either conduct a reappraisal using only in-house staff or hire external consultants to do some or all of the required appraisal work. The process involves what is known as a mass appraisal, meaning not every parcel of real property is inspected by appraisers. Usually a small representative sample of a county's real property will be individually appraised. The rest of the county's real property will be assigned tax values based on an analysis of market prices and physical characteristics at the neighborhood level.

Changes to Real Property Tax Values in Non-Reappraisal Years

In between reappraisals, real property tax values generally should change only due to physical or zoning changes to the property. Changes in general economic conditions or in the local real estate market should not be reflected in tax values until the next reappraisal.

For example, assume that Billy BlueDevil owns Parcel A that was appraised at $300,000 in Carolina County's 2008 reappraisal. The county's next reappraisal is not scheduled until 2016. Billy sells Parcel A to Tommy TarHeel in 2012 for $200,000 in an arms-length, non-foreclosure transaction. Although the true market value of Parcel A may be $200,000 as of 2012, the tax value of Parcel A should not change until the next reappraisal in 2016. The tax value of Parcel A must remain its true market value as of January 1, 2008. The same would be true if Billy's house sold in 2012 for more than its 2008 tax value.

Now assume that instead of selling Parcel A, Billy increases the size of his house on that lot by 2,000 square feet in 2012. This physical change to Parcel A should be reflected in the 2013 tax value of Parcel A. The 2013 tax value would also need to be changed if Billy's house burned down in 2012 or if Parcel A were rezoned in 2012 to make it more or less valuable for future development or use.

Public Service Company Property

Only one type of property is assessed at the state level: real and personal property owned by electricity providers, gas companies, railroads, telephone service providers, and other public service companies.

Each year these companies are required to list their taxable property with the N.C. Department of Revenue, which then assigns a tax value to that property and allocates that value to local governments for taxation. For real property such as a power plant, the allocation is based on location. For movable personal property such as buses and trains, the allocation is based on the miles driven in a jurisdiction, the miles of track in a jurisdiction, or a similar formula. If a local government's sales assessment ratio falls below 90 percent in certain years, that local government can lose a percentage of its public service company property value. See the next section for more on sales assessment ratios.

Once public service company property value has been allocated to a local government, it may tax that property just as it taxes all other property in its jurisdiction. Unlike regular property tax appeals, appeals of public service company property tax values go directly to the state Property Tax Commission and are not handled at the county level.

Sales Assessment Ratios

Each year the N.C. Department of Revenue studies a sample of real estate sales from each county and compares the sales prices to the property tax appraisals of the sold properties. Foreclosures and other transactions that were not arms-length transactions are excluded from these studies. A ratio is created for each property by dividing the tax appraisal by the sales price. The median of all of the ratios is that county's sales assessment ratio.

This ratio is a rough measure of how closely the county's tax values reflect actual market values. Ideally the ratio would be 100 percent, meaning that on average tax appraisals are pegged right at market values. If the ratio is below 100 percent, then tax appraisals are below market values. If the ratio is greater than 100 percent, then tax appraisals are above market values.

In normal economic times, sales assessment ratios decrease in the years following appraisals because tax values remain basically constant while market values slowly but steadily increase. When a county conducts its reappraisal, its sales assessment ratio will jump back up close to 100 percent. Only a handful of counties will have ratios over 100 percent, usually those few who have just conducted reappraisals and pegged their tax values slightly above the market.

Sadly, North Carolina has not experienced normal economic times since 2008. While most real property markets in the state have avoided the huge booms and busts witnessed in cities such as Las Vegas or Miami, on average home prices in North Carolina have fallen in the past few years. As of late 2011, the average price of existing homes in North Carolina was down about 15 percent from its peak in 2007.

As a result, in 2010 an increasing number of counties began to experience rising sales assessment ratios. In 2012 more than two-thirds of North Carolina counties had ratios over 100 percent. Clay County led the pack with a sales assessment ratio of 142 percent, meaning that its tax values were on average 40 percent higher than market value.

This unprecedented state of affairs means that some local governments can expect to experience a drop in their tax bases after their next reappraisals. Currituck County, for example, saw its tax base drop more than 20 percent after its 2011 reappraisal. Some beach communities in Onslow County that benefitted from a booming real estate market in the mid-2000s suffered drops of more than 40 percent after the county's 2010 reappraisal.

When a jurisdiction's tax base shrinks, it must either reduce spending or raise its tax rate. Currituck County's tax rate, long the lowest in the state, jumped from $.23 in 2010 to $.30 in 2011 as a result of its reappraisal.

Most counties will not see such dramatic decreases in their tax bases, of course. But the lesson of the past few years is that local governments can no longer count on healthy increases in their tax bases—and corresponding drops in their tax rates—after every reappraisal.

Why the Sales Assessment Ratio Matters

County leaders can use the sales assessment ratio to evaluate the effectiveness of their reappraisals. The ratio can also help predict how the county's tax base will change in the next reappraisal: if a county's sales assessment ratio is well above 100 percent, county leaders should be prepared for a drop in the tax base after the next reappraisal.

There are statutory reasons to pay attention to the sales assessment ratio as well. It is the basis for two Machinery Act provisions intended to promote more frequent appraisals of real property.

The first provision deals with public service company property. If a county's sales assessment ratio falls below 90 percent in the fourth or seventh year after a reappraisal, then that county's assessed value of public service company property will be reduced. The reduction will roughly equate to the actual sales assessment ratio: if the county's ratio is 85 percent, the county will be allocated and will be able to tax only 85 percent of the full assessed value of the public service company property it would otherwise have been allocated.

The second provision involves mandatory reappraisals for counties with populations greater than 75,000. If such a county's sales assessment ratio is below 85 percent or above 115 percent, then the county must conduct a reappraisal within three years.

Although the mandatory reappraisal provision has been in place since 2008, it has been triggered only once. In 2012 Union County's sales assessment ratio rose to 119 percent, and the county was required to move its next reappraisal from 2016 to 2015. The statute's lack of use is partly due to the population restriction, which exempts one-third of the state's 100 counties from its scope. But the three-year grace period also plays a large part: by the time a county's ratio reaches more than 15 percent off of market value, that county is likely to already be within three years of its next reappraisal.

Property Tax Exemptions and Exclusions

Only the General Assembly has the authority to create exemptions from local property taxes. Local governments may not carve out their own exemptions nor may they choose not to administer the exemptions created by the General Assembly.

As Figure 5 illustrates, the single largest property tax exemption is the one for property owned by a government—federal, state, or local. Local governments have no authority to tax property owned by another branch of government, regardless of how that property is being used.

Figure 5.   North Carolina Taxable Property and Exempted Property, 2010–2011

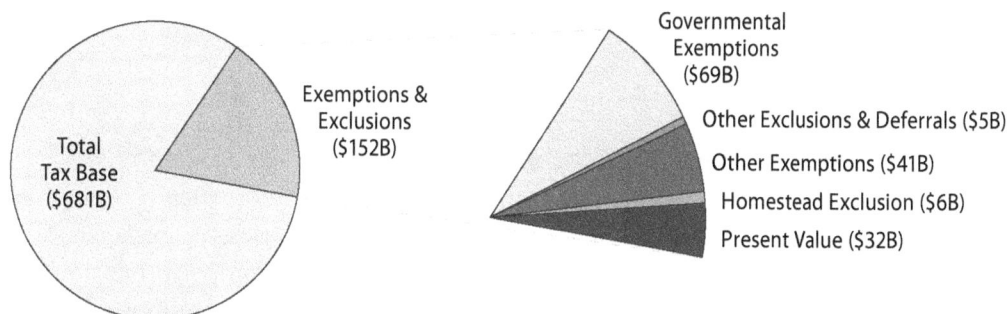

Total Tax Base ($681B)

Exemptions & Exclusions ($152B)

Governmental Exemptions ($69B)

Other Exclusions & Deferrals ($5B)

Other Exemptions ($41B)

Homestead Exclusion ($6B)

Present Value ($32B)

Source: N.C. Department of Revenue

The second largest exemption is the present-use value (PUV) deferred tax program for farmland and forestland. Under this program, farmers and foresters are allowed to pay taxes on the value of their property at its value for agricultural use as opposed to its actual market value for development or any other use. The taxes on the difference between the PUV and the market value are deferred, with the most recent three years of deferred taxes due and payable when the property is sold or is no longer used as farmland or forestland.

Three residential property exclusions are aimed specifically at elderly and disabled home owners. The most popular of the three is the homestead exclusion, which reduces the taxable value of a residence by the greater of $25,000 or 50 percent. To be eligible the owner must be sixty-five or older or totally disabled and must satisfy an income requirement, which was $27,100 or less for 2012. For example, if Tina Taxpayer is eligible for the elderly and disabled exclusion and her home is assessed at $200,000, she will pay taxes only on $100,000 of that value.

The other two exclusions are the disabled veterans exclusion, which allows qualified taxpayers to reduce the taxable value of their homes by $45,000, and the circuit breaker deferred tax program, which permits taxpayers to cap their current taxes at either 4 or 5 percent of their income. The circuit breaker program is similar to the PUV program in that three years of deferred circuit breaker taxes are due when the taxpayer sells the home or stops using it as his or her primary residence.

Other common exemptions cover property used for religious, educational, and charitable purposes, non-business personal property (individual taxpayers' televisions, computers, furniture, baseball card collections, and the like), and business inventory.

Exemption and Exclusion Applications

Property owned by a government or a governmental agency is automatically exempt. All other property owners must submit applications to receive exemptions or exclusions.

Most exemptions and exclusions require only a single application per property. Additional filings by the taxpayer are required only if an exempt taxpayer acquires additional property, makes physical changes to the exempt property, or changes its use of the exempt property.

A few exclusions require annual applications. Most notable among this group is the circuit breaker program, which bases its tax break on the taxpayer's income for the previous calendar year.

Applications for most exemptions and exclusions are due by the end of the listing period, which is January 31 unless the county commissioners decide to extend it. Applications for the three residential property relief programs—the elderly and disabled exclusion, the circuit breaker exclusion, and the disabled veterans exclusion—are due on June 1.

Despite these deadlines, the Machinery Act permits governing boards to accept applications though December 31 for "good cause shown." Because this term is not defined by the Machinery Act, governing boards have a good amount of discretion when deciding which late applications to consider. The only limitation courts have placed on this discretion is that local governments should not base their decisions solely on the amount of property taxes related to a particular application.

The assessor makes the initial determination on all exemption and exclusion applications. North Carolina courts have made clear that all exemptions and exclusions must be strictly construed in favor of taxation. In other words, assessors should begin with a presumption in favor of taxability. The burden of proof is on the taxpayer to prove that an exemption or exclusion is deserved. If the taxpayer disagrees with the assessor's decision concerning an exemption or exclusion, the taxpayer may pursue an appeal to the county board of equalization and review and beyond, as described below.

Taxpayer Appeals

County commissioners play significant roles in resolving taxpayer appeals concerning their tax values and their eligibility for exemptions or exclusions, primarily through the appointment of the county board of equalization and review (BOER). The commissioners themselves may sit as the BOER or, as is most common, they may appoint other individuals to serve in that capacity.

Confusingly, the Machinery Act does not create a fixed deadline for taxpayers to submit appeals to the BOER. Instead, the appeal deadline is tied to the date that the BOER adjourns, which can vary from county to county and from year to year.

In non-reappraisal years, the BOER must adjourn by July 1. In reappraisal years, it must do so by December 1. But in practice, most counties adjourn their BOERs on the same day as or shortly after the BOER's first meeting, which must occur between the first Monday in April and the first Monday in May. Once it adjourns, the BOER may still meet to hear appeals that were submitted before adjournment but cannot accept any new appeals.

Table 5 lists the five stages of a property tax appeal. Not surprisingly, most appeals occur in reappraisal years when every parcel of real property receives a new tax value. Historically, about 10 percent of real property owners contest their values after a reappraisal. The assessor usually resolves 90 percent of those initial inquiries informally.

The remaining 10 percent may, at the discretion of the taxpayer, move to the BOER for formal appeal hearings. The BOER's decision is binding on the county, meaning that if the taxpayer prevails, the county has no right of appeal. However, if the county prevails, the taxpayer has the right to appeal to the North Carolina Property Tax Commission, a five-member panel that hears cases in Raleigh. The party that loses before the Property Tax Commissioner can appeal the case to the North Carolina Court of Appeals, which is often the final stop for property tax appeals. A losing party has the right to continue its appeal to the North Carolina Supreme Court only if at least one judge from the court of appeals

Table 5. The Property Tax Appeal Process

1. Informal Appeal to the Assessor
2. County Board of Equalization and Review
3. State Property Tax Commission (taxpayer only)
4. N.C. Court of Appeals
5. N.C. Supreme Court (maybe)

voted in its favor. The supreme court may also exercise its discretion to hear the appeal of a unanimous decision from the court of appeals, but that rarely occurs.

Discoveries

A "discovery" occurs when the assessor learns of taxable property that has not been listed for property taxes. The term also applies when the value or volume of property was substantially understated or when a property has received an exemption or exclusion for which it did not qualify.

After a discovery is made, the assessor must correct the listing and assessment of the property and then bill the corrected taxes for the current year plus the five previous years. If the discovery involves personal property or buildings, discovery penalties of 10 percent per listing period apply to the discovery bill. Penalties do not apply to the failure to list land.

For example, assume that Billy BlueDevil builds a house on his vacant lot in 2005 but fails to list the building for taxation with the county. The county finally learns of the house's existence in 2012. Under the discovery provisions, the county is entitled to list, assess, and bill that property for the current year (2012), plus the five previous years (2007–2011). Although the house should have been listed and taxed in 2006, the Machinery Act does not permit the county to extend its discovery bill back past 2007.

The discovery bill must be based on the assessed value and the tax rate in effect for each year the property was not listed. Table 6 shows how Billy BlueDevil's discovery bill would look, assuming that the house would have been assessed at $200,000 as of January 1, 2007, and that the county had not conducted a reappraisal since that date. The penalties are calculated at 10 percent per missed listing period for each tax year: for example, the 2007 penalty is 60 percent because Billy missed six listing periods (2007–2012).

Waiving Discovery Bills

Local governing boards possess unusually broad authority when it comes to discovery bills. The Machinery Act permits discovery bills to be waived by the governing board for any reason whatsoever. The governing board may agree to waive the entire bill or just a portion. It could waive all penalties, or the tax and penalties from certain years, or any combination thereof.

In comparison, regular tax bills, penalties, and interest generally cannot be waived by governing boards. See "Refunds and Releases," below, for more details.

Table 6. Discovery Bill for 2012 Discovery of $200,000 House

Year	Assessed Value	Tax Rate	Tax	Penalty	Totals
2012	$200,000	.51	$1,020	$102 (10%)	$1,122
2011	$200,000	.51	$1,020	$204 (20%)	$1,224
2010	$200,000	.50	$1,000	$300 (30%)	$1,300
2009	$200,000	.52	$1,040	$416 (40%)	$1,456
2008	$200,000	.52	$1,040	$520 (50%)	$1,560
2007	$200,000	.50	$1,000	$600 (60%)	$1,600
Totals			$6,120	$2,142	$8,262

While the Machinery Act does not place any specific limits on the authority to waive discovery bills, governing boards are wise to seek consistency in their approaches to this issue. A lack of consistency when making waiver decisions could lead to accusations of favoritism or bias.

When the discovery bill includes municipal property taxes, that municipality's governing board retains the authority to compromise that portion of the bill. The county commissioners may compromise only the portion of the discovery bill that involves county taxes.

Evaluating the Assessor

County commissioners can choose from a variety of metrics to evaluate the performance of their assessors. One major consideration is often the cost and effectiveness of the countywide reappraisal of real property. Reappraisals are usually the most controversial activity undertaken by the tax office. To conduct a successful reappraisal, an assessor must possess technical appraisal skills, managerial competence, and perhaps above all, strong public relations capability. Educating taxpayers about the reappraisal and appeal process is a necessity, and the assessor cannot accomplish that key task without the ability to communicate clearly and effectively to different interest groups.

From a statistical perspective, the sales assessment ratio may be the most useful figure for the county commissioners to analyze. Immediately following a reappraisal, the county's sales assessment figure should be very close to 100 percent, meaning that on average sales prices equal tax values. If that is not the case, the reappraisal was not very accurate and the assessor should be held accountable.

The assessor should not be held accountable for changes in the tax base due to economic conditions. The fact that tax values have not risen as much as the commissioners might have hoped or have not fallen as much as taxpayers might have expected does not mean that the assessor is incompetent. More often, it means that the observers' expectations were not based on the actual conditions experienced by the county. Pre-reappraisal education is the key to minimizing unrealistic expectations on behalf of both elected officials and taxpayers.

Questions for Discussion

1. When was your county's last reappraisal of real property? When is the next one scheduled? What advantages and disadvantages come with this schedule?

2. What was your county's most recent sales assessment ratio? How does this compare to previous years and to similar jurisdictions?

3. What is the total assessed value of taxable property in your local government's jurisdiction? What was the total dollar value of deferred taxes?

4. Does your board of county commissioners also serve as the board of equalization and review? What are the advantages and disadvantages of this arrangement?

5. How does your county's assessor inform taxpayers of the availability of the three property tax exclusions focused on residential property: the elderly and disabled exclusion, the circuit breaker exclusion, and the disabled veterans exclusion?

Collection

After the assessor lists and assesses all taxable property in the jurisdiction and the governing board sets the tax rate, property taxes are handed over to the tax collector for billing and, if necessary, enforced collection efforts such as bank account attachments, wage garnishments, and real property foreclosures.

As is true of the listing and assessing process, the collection process should normally proceed with minimal involvement by the governing board. The tax collector should apply the same collection procedures to all similarly situated taxpayers, free from political pressures.

The governing board's role in the collection process is limited to

- appointing a tax collector or, for municipalities, choosing to contract with the county for property tax collection;
- deciding whether to offer taxpayers a discount for early payment; and
- reviewing the tax collector's performance throughout the year and after receiving the year-end settlement.

Appointing the Tax Collector

Every local government that levies property taxes must appoint a tax collector who will be authorized to use the Machinery Act collection remedies of attachment and garnishment, levy and sale, and foreclosure. That tax collector can be an employee of the taxing government or an employee of another government with whom the taxing government contracts for tax collection services.

The Machinery Act creates only a few limitations on who can be appointed as tax collector. Members of the governing board are ineligible to serve as tax collector, as are local government finance officers absent special approval from the Local Government Commission. In terms of education and experience, the only requirement is that the appointee be "a person of character and integrity whose experience in business and collection work is satisfactory to the governing body." The appointee's criminal and financial history must not be so bad as to prevent the local government from being able to purchase the required bond to cover losses caused by the tax collector's misconduct or neglect. The bottom line is that the governing body has great discretion when deciding whom to appoint as tax collector.

The tax collector must be appointed for a set term determined by the governing board. Most commonly these terms are two or four years in length. Once fixed by the governing board upon the tax collector' appointment, the length of the collector's term may not be changed until the term ends or the collector is removed from office. No term limits exist for collectors, meaning the governing board may reappoint a particular tax collector repeatedly. After appointment, the tax collector can be removed from office only "for cause," the same standard that is applied to the removal of the assessor.

Unlike assessors, tax collectors are not subject to mandatory state certification. However, the North Carolina Tax Collectors Association (NCTCA) operates a voluntary certification process for tax collectors. Many local governments now expect their collectors to obtain NCTCA certification as part of their required duties.

Tax Bills

Surprisingly, the Machinery Act does not require local governments that levy property taxes to send bills to their taxpayers. For obvious reasons, all do. But because tax bills are not required, a taxpayer cannot rely on failure to receive a tax bill as justification to avoid responsibility for a particular tax. The Machinery Act charges all taxpayers with notice of the fact that taxes are owed on their property even if they never receive actual notice in the form of a tax bill.

Tax bills cannot be created until the tax rate is adopted along with the budget for the new fiscal year. Local governments are expected to finalize their budgets before July 1, the beginning of the fiscal year. But this deadline is far from ironclad, and plenty of local governments delay the final budget decision well into the new fiscal year. Of course, the later the budget is adopted, the later tax bills will go out, and the longer the local government will wait to receive its property tax revenue.

Because the Machinery Act is silent on the issue of tax bills, local governments have flexibility as to the form and content of those bills. Any tax, fee, fine or other obligation can be included on a property tax bill. But billing an obligation along with property taxes does not automatically empower the local government to use property tax collection remedies to collect that obligation.

Should cities and towns collect their own taxes?

All 100 counties appoint and employ their own tax collectors. So do many municipalities. But a growing number of municipalities have decided not to employ their own tax collectors and instead have appointed the county tax collector as the municipal tax collector through interlocal agreements.

The Machinery Act offers no guidance on the terms of these city–county collection agreements, meaning that the compensation provided by the city to the county for its tax collection services is up for negotiation between the parties. The compensation typically is set as a percentage of the taxes collected, usually around 1 to 2 percent and sometimes with a bonus if the collection rate exceeds a certain benchmark.

From a financial perspective, relying on the county tax collector makes sense for many municipalities. The county already has the billing infrastructure in place, meaning that the cost it charges to the municipality to bill and collect municipal taxes will likely be less than the cost the municipality would incur to create its own billing system. But some municipalities prefer to retain complete control over the billing and collection process even if that approach costs more in the long run.

For example, some local governments include water, sewer, or stormwater fees on their tax bills. Absent special approval from the state legislature, these fees cannot be collected using property tax collection remedies even though they are included on the same bill with property taxes.

An important exception to this rule concerns solid waste fees. All local governments are authorized to adopt a resolution calling for solid waste fees to be billed with property taxes and collected as property taxes.

Discounts for Early Payment

The Machinery Act permits but does not require local governments to offer taxpayers a discount for paying their property taxes before September 1, the due date for property taxes other than those on registered motor vehicles. Discounts are becoming less and less common. Those jurisdictions that do offer them usually set the discount at 1 or 2 percent. If a jurisdiction wishes to offer a discount, it must set the discount schedule by May and obtain approval from the N.C. Department of Revenue. Once adopted, a discount schedule remains in effect for all subsequent tax years unless and until it is repealed by the governing board.

Interest

Unlike discounts, interest is mandatory. On January 6 following the year in which the taxes are levied, unpaid property taxes begin to accrue interest. For example, taxes levied for the 2011–2012 fiscal year became delinquent and began to accrue interest on January 6, 2012. (Different rules apply to taxes on motor vehicles—see "Registered Motor Vehicles," below.)

Interest accrues at a rate of 2 percent for the first month and 0.75 percent for every month thereafter. Machinery Act interest is simple interest rather than compound interest, meaning that interest does not accrue on interest. On the first day of each month that a delinquent tax remains unpaid, another 0.75 percent of interest accrues on the principal amount of taxes owed plus any penalties and costs that have been added to that amount. For example, tax collectors are permitted to apply a 10 percent penalty for checks returned by the bank for insufficient funds. That penalty is added to the principal amount of taxes owed and will accrue interest if it remains unpaid past the delinquency date.

Governing boards cannot waive interest charges unless that interest accrued illegally or due to clerical error. These are the same standards that apply to the release and refund of principal taxes—see "Refunds and Releases," below, for more details.

Special Rules: Weekends, Holidays, and Postmarks

Two Machinery Act provisions affect when interest accrues in special situations.

The first is the weekend and holiday rule. Whenever the last day to pay a tax without additional interest falls on a weekend or holiday, the deadline is extended to the next business day. For example, January 6, 2013, falls on a Sunday, meaning the last day to pay 2012–2013 property taxes without interest falls on a Saturday (January 5). The weekend and holiday rule extends this deadline to the next business day (Monday, January 7). Interest on unpaid 2012–2013 property taxes will not accrue until Tuesday, January 8.

The second is the postmark rule. The Machinery Act requires that tax offices treat property tax payments made by mail as if the payments were received on their postmark dates. Assume Tommy TarHeel pays his 2012–2013 property taxes in full by mail on Monday, January 7, 2013. The tax office does not receive his payment until Wednesday, January 9, the day after interest was to accrue on 2012–2013 property taxes. If Tommy's payment has a postmark date of Monday, January 7, the tax office must treat the payment as if it were actually received on that date. No interest would accrue on Tommy's property taxes.

Depending on the size of the locality, it may not be practical for tax office staff to check postmark dates on all payments made on or near an interest deadline. Instead, many tax offices apply a grace period of several days after each interest accrual date. Payments received by mail within the grace period do not accrue interest, without regard for post-mark dates. While reasonable, tax offices should be aware that this practice satisfies only the spirit and not the letter of the postmark rule. Tax payments arriving after the grace period that have postmark dates prior to the interest accrual date should not be charged interest.

Deferred Taxes

At least seven different Machinery Act provisions provide taxpayers tax relief in the form of deferred taxes. By far the largest of these deferred tax programs is the present-use value program covering farmland. But deferred tax programs also cover residential property under the circuit breaker program, as well as historic properties, new homes owned by builders, working waterfront property, wildlife conservation land, and future sites for low-income housing.

The details of these programs vary, but the general principle remains the same: some amount of taxes is deferred each year for as long as the property qualifies for the program. Interest accrues on these deferred taxes, but the local government cannot take action to collect them. When the property is sold or otherwise becomes ineligible for the program, several years (usually three) of deferred taxes plus interest become due and payable. If the deferred taxes are not paid immediately, the local government can proceed with enforced collection remedies.

Enforced Collection Remedies

Once taxes become delinquent on January 6, tax collectors can begin enforced collections immediately. The Machinery Act creates three enforced collection remedies: attachment and garnishment; levy and sale; and, for taxes that are liens on real property, foreclosure.

Table 7. Enforced Collection Remedies

Remedy	Property Targeted
Attachment and garnishment	Wages, bank accounts, rents, or any other money owed to the taxpayer
Levy and sale	Cars, boats, planes, or any other tangible personal property owned by the taxpayer
Foreclosure	Real property subject to a lien for delinquent taxes
Set-off debt collection	State income tax refunds, lottery winnings, or any other money owed to the taxpayer by the state

Separate state provisions allow local governments to collect delinquent property taxes through the set-off debt collection process, which targets state income tax refunds and lottery winnings. All four remedies are summarized in Table 7.

Local governments can also sue delinquent taxpayers in state court, but few pursue this option because the remedies available to the local government after winning such a lawsuit are essentially the same remedies it already possesses under the Machinery Act.

Unless the governing board directs otherwise, the tax collector normally may use any of these remedies in any order desired. However, once a foreclosure proceeding begins, all other Machinery Act remedies must stop.

Most local governments use all four tax collection remedies. But some refuse to employ collection remedies that taxpayers consider too intrusive, such as wage garnishment or foreclosure. Local governments that ignore any of these remedies suffer reduced collection percentages and lost revenues and do grievous harm to the perceived fairness of the property tax scheme.

Three of these remedies can be initiated without the involvement of the courts. Attachment and garnishment, levy and sale, and set-off debt collection require only notice to the taxpayer and, in the case of attachment and garnishment, notice to the party that holds the property being attached.

A court proceeding is required for foreclosure, which is available only for taxes that are a lien on real property. All taxes on real property automatically become a lien on that real property on the listing date, which is the January 1 prior to the fiscal year for which the taxes are levied. The tax lien on real property also includes the taxes owed on personal property other than registered motor vehicles that is owned by the same taxpayer in the same jurisdiction.

For example, assume that Wanda Wolfpack owns real property Parcel A, a boat, and a registered Honda Civic, all of which are listed for taxes in Carolina County. The taxes on both Parcel A and the boat are a lien on Parcel A. The county could foreclose on Parcel A for Wanda's failure to pay either the taxes on the real property itself or the taxes on the boat. The taxes on the Honda Civic are *not* a lien on Parcel A, meaning that the tax collector could not foreclose on Parcel A if Wanda failed to pay the taxes on her Civic.

The Machinery Act creates a ten-year statute of limitations for all enforced collections. Foreclosures, attachments and garnishments, and levies must begin within ten years of the delinquent tax's original due date, which for all taxes other than those on registered motor vehicles is September 1 of the year the taxes were levied.

Who Can Be Targeted with Enforced Collection Remedies?

Only property of the responsible taxpayer can be targeted with enforced collection remedies. Responsibility for taxes on real property follows the property. New owners of real property are personally responsible for old taxes on that real property. For taxes on personal property, responsibility usually lies only with the taxpayer that listed the property for the delinquent taxes—new owners of personal property are not responsible for old taxes on that property. Table 8 summarizes the rules concerning responsible taxpayers.

Here is how the rules work for real property. Assume that Dave Deacon owns Parcel A, on which taxes from 2011–2012 are delinquent. He sells Parcel A to Susie Seahawk. Normally Susie (or her attorney) would require that the delinquent taxes be paid at or before the closing. But if those taxes are not paid, Susie would be personally responsible for the old taxes on Parcel A despite the fact that the taxes became delinquent while the property was owned by Dave. Dave would also remain personally responsible. To collect these taxes, the tax collector could foreclose on Parcel A, garnish Dave's or Susie's wages, attach Dave's or Susie's bank account, or seize and sell Dave's or Susie's car or other personal property. If Susie's cash or property is taken to satisfy the taxes, Susie may have a legal action against Dave for reimbursement. But that depends on the terms of the real estate contract between Susie and Dave and has no effect on the taxing unit's right to collect the delinquent taxes using all methods permitted by the Machinery Act.

Now consider a personal property example. Assume that Dave Deacon owns a Ford Fusion on which 2012 property taxes are delinquent. If Dave sells the Ford to Susie Seahawk, then only Dave will remain personally responsible. Only Dave's wages, bank accounts, and other property may be targeted with enforced collections. The tax collector cannot seize and sell the car or target any of Susie's other property, because responsibility for taxes on that car does not transfer to its new owner.

Although multiple collection actions are permitted for a single delinquent tax, that tax may be collected only once. Assume that in the Ford Fusion example the tax collector

Table 8. Which Owners Can Be Held Personally Responsible for Property Taxes?

Type of Property	Original Owner	Subsequent Owners
Real property	Yes	Yes
Personal property (boats, planes, business property)	Yes	No, unless "going-out-of-business" provision applies
Registered motor vehicles	Yes	No

garnished Dave's wages for the delinquent taxes and also attached Dave's bank account for the taxes owed on the Ford. The tax collector is permitted to move forward with both collection actions simultaneously. But once the full delinquent tax plus interest and costs are collected, all collection actions must stop and any excess funds collected must be returned to the taxpayer.

There is one situation in which the new owner of personal property may be held liable for old taxes on that property. The special "going-out-of-business" provisions apply when business personal property such as factory equipment is sold by a business that is closing or changing ownership. The buyer of that equipment is responsible for all existing taxes on that property. The tax collector can use Machinery Act remedies against the buyer to collect those taxes if such remedies begin within six months of the sale. After that period, the tax collector's only collection option is to sue the buyer in state court.

Property Taxes and the Register of Deeds

More than two-thirds of North Carolina's 100 counties have received authorization from the General Assembly to prohibit the register of deeds from accepting a deed transferring real property unless the tax collector first certifies that there are no property tax liens on the property that is the subject of the deed. This certification must cover all property taxes that the county tax collector is responsible for collecting, which could include county taxes, municipal taxes, special service district taxes, rural fire district taxes, and supplemental school district taxes. This provision provides great incentive for the closing attorney to ensure that the taxes are paid, because otherwise the deed cannot be recorded and the buyer's ownership rights may be jeopardized. Unfortunately, the provision contains a loophole that permits attorneys to record deeds if they promise to pay the delinquent taxes at closing. Too often these promises are broken and the taxes remain unpaid after the deeds are recorded.

G.S. 161-31 lists the counties with the authority to enact this requirement. If a county is not on that list and desires this authority, it should ask its state representatives to introduce legislation adding it to that list. Although the statute covers municipal taxes only if those taxes are collected by the county, at least one city that collects its own taxes has obtained a local modification to the law that prohibits the recording of deeds unless city taxes are paid along with the county taxes.

Advertising Tax Liens

Despite increasing questions about their effectiveness, newspaper advertisements of delinquent real property tax liens are still required every year. The cost of these advertisements can be substantial, with larger counties spending tens of thousands of dollars to buy newspaper space. Tax collectors are permitted to pass these costs along to the delinquent taxpayers, and much of the advertising cost will be recaptured when the delinquent taxes are paid. But because not all of these taxes will be paid, the local government is certain to wind up eating a portion of the advertising cost.

Due to cost and to administrative burden, some local governments have considered eliminating tax lien advertisements. This course of action is not recommended for two reasons.

First, the advertisement is the mandatory initial step for an *in rem* foreclosure, the Machinery Act's expedited foreclosure process that can be accomplished without the need for attorneys. If a tax collector were to move forward with an *in rem* foreclosure without first advertising the tax lien, the taxpayer would have strong grounds for defending or reversing that collection action.

Second, local governments that do not use the *in rem* foreclosure process could place their other collection actions at risk if they intentionally ignore the advertising requirement. While the Machinery Act and state courts are generally tolerant of good faith errors in the tax collection process (see the discussion under "Immaterial Irregularities," below), they are less likely to be forgiving of willful illegality by a local government.

Evaluating the Tax Collector: The Tax Collection Percentage

The Machinery Act requires tax collectors to make monthly reports to their governing boards about their collection results. These reports, combined with the annual settlement required of tax collectors summing up their efforts and results for the entire fiscal year, give governing boards multiple opportunities to evaluate the performance of their collectors.

Table 9.   Property Tax Collection Percentages, 2011

	Counties	Municipalities
All taxes	97.19%	97.42%
Taxes on registered motor vehicles only	87.23%	86.41%

Source: N.C. Department of State Treasurer

Perhaps the most important statistic used in the evaluation process is the tax collection percentage. Thanks to the very effective collection remedies provided by the Machinery Act, on average collection percentages are very high. Table 9 summarizes the average percentages for counties and municipalities. Collections of taxes on registered motor vehicles have always lagged behind collections of other property taxes. See "Registered Motor Vehicles," below, for more details on the billing and collection process for motor vehicle taxes and how that will likely change in 2013.

Two factors that can affect an individual local government's collection percentage are property tax assessment appeals and bankruptcies, both of which prevent a tax collector from pursuing enforced collections against the taxpayer in question. If a jurisdiction experiences either a high number of property tax appeals during a reappraisal year or a bankruptcy filing by a major commercial taxpayer, the tax collector will not be able to collect the taxes involved while the proceedings are pending. As a result, the collection percentage is likely to suffer.

"Settlement" is the term the Machinery Act uses for the required annual accounting that the tax collector must provide to the local governing board. Presented after the old fiscal year ends and before the tax collector is charged with taxes for the new fiscal year, the settlement accounts for all of the funds received by the tax collector and identifies those taxes that remain unpaid. The settlement must be provided to the board in written form, but most tax collectors also make an oral presentation to the governing board so that they can answer questions in person.

As part of the settlement, the tax collector will usually provide the governing board with multiple settlement percentages. These percentages often include one for all property taxes from the just-ended fiscal year, one for registered motor vehicle taxes for the just-ended fiscal year, one for prior years' taxes, and one for prior years' taxes on registered motor vehicles.

Other Performance Evaluation Measures

Although collection percentage is the most common and usually the most important criterion used to evaluate a tax collector, other aspects of the collector's performance can and should be considered by the board. The collector's ability to communicate with the board and with the public is key to an effective property tax system. Taxpayer complaints and the collector's responsiveness to those complaints are related issues that may provide insight into that official's performance.

Consistency and impartiality are vital characteristics for a tax collector. The board needs proof that the collector demonstrates these traits. Does the tax collector treat all similarly situated taxpayers equally? Is he or she employing tax collection remedies in an impartial fashion against all delinquent taxpayers and not playing favorites? If not, the local government is likely to face taxpayer dissatisfaction and legal exposure.

Old Taxes

The Machinery Act creates a ten-year statute of limitations that bars enforced collection actions after taxes are more than ten years past due. Most counties rely on this statute of limitations to allow the tax collector to write off taxes after they hit the ten-year mark. Technically, this approach violates the Machinery Act. The statute of limitations bars enforced collection, but it has no relevance to the tax collector's responsibility for those taxes.

The only technically correct method of writing off taxes and thereby relieving the tax collector of responsibility for them is through the "insolvents list." As part of the settlement process, the tax collector should identify unpaid taxes from the just-ended fiscal year that are not a lien on real property. The governing board can then place those taxes on the insolvents list and, once those taxes are more than five years past due, can write off those taxes by relieving the tax collector of responsibility for them. Taxes on registered motor vehicles that are placed on the insolvents list can be written off after they are more than one year past due.

Note that taxes that are a lien on real property cannot be placed on the insolvents list and therefore technically can never be written off by the tax collector. When all other efforts fail, foreclosure remains an option for any tax that is secured by a lien on real property. The problem is, property that makes it through to a foreclosure sale is often worth very little. It may be more effort than it is worth to pursue foreclosure, which is why many counties allow the tax collector to informally write off old taxes on real property despite the Machinery Act's contrary admonition.

Immaterial Irregularities—
the Machinery Act's "Get-Out-Of-Jail-Free Card"

From a local government perspective, there are few Machinery Act provisions more beneficial than the "immaterial irregularity" provision. Essentially, this provision excuses errors in the listing, assessing, billing, and collecting processes and allows local governments to retroactively correct those errors and levy and collect the taxes in question as if the errors never occurred.

Cities and counties have relied on the immaterial irregularity provision in a variety of situations. They have used it to retroactively bill taxes on property that was listed by the taxpayer but never assessed, to pursue taxes on property that was annexed by a city years ago but never taxed by the city, and to collect underbillings that resulted from computer errors.

About the only type of error that courts have found significant enough not to be excused is the failure to give adequate notice to owners of real property before moving forward with a foreclosure action. Local governments using the foreclosure process should take care to provide timely notice to all parties who may have an interest in the property being foreclosed upon, including lien holders and the heirs of deceased taxpayers.

Questions for Discussion

1. Does your local government offer a discount for early payment of property taxes? If so, how much of a discount?

2. Which of these enforced collection remedies does your tax collector regularly use?

   a. Attachment and garnishment of wages and bank accounts

   b. Levy and sale

   c. Foreclosure

   d. Set-off debt collection

3. What was your local government's most recent property tax collection percentage?

Refunds and Releases

A favorite question from taxpayers, tax collectors, and governing boards across the state is, when can taxes be waived? The short answer is, very rarely. Governing boards cannot waive taxes whenever they choose.

In Machinery Act terminology, waivers are either "refunds" (for taxes that were previously paid) or "releases" (for taxes that have not been paid). Under G.S. 105-381, refunds and releases are permitted in only two circumstances:

1. when the tax was levied illegally, or
2. when the tax was levied due to clerical error by the tax office.

If a board approves a refund or release that does not satisfy one of these two categories, the board members can be held personally liable for the lost taxes.

Examples of illegal taxes include

- taxes on property that did not have situs in the jurisdiction,
- double taxation on the same property by the same jurisdiction, and
- taxes that were levied without the required procedural steps.

Examples of taxes levied due to clerical error include

- assessments in which figures were transposed (for example, a tax value of $250,000 is mistakenly recorded as $520,000);
- tax payments applied to the wrong accounts contrary to taxpayer instructions or due to mistakes by the tax office; and
- tax bills calculated on the wrong tax rate.

Two of the most common reasons taxpayers seek refunds and releases *do not* satisfy G.S. 105-381. Governing boards should not approve tax waiver requests based on either

1. value judgments by the assessor's office, or
2. clerical errors made by the taxpayer rather than by the tax office.

First, consider value judgments made by the assessor. These judgments must be challenged during the regular appeal process that closes when the county board of equalization and review adjourns. (See "Listing and Assessing," above.) Otherwise, a local government would have great difficulties budgeting each year because its tax base would always be subject to retroactive adjustments due to after-the-fact value appeals. These errors in judgment can be corrected going forward so that future tax bills are accurate, but retroactive changes are not permitted.

The best question to ask when deciding if a mistake by the tax office was a value judgment or a clerical error is, was the resulting assessment the one intended by the assessor? If so, then the issue is a value judgment that cannot justify a refund or release. If not, then the issue is a clerical error that can justify a refund or release.

For example, consider two houses that were each assessed at $400,000 during Carolina County's last reappraisal in 2010.

House A was intended to be assessed at a square footage of 2,500, but a data entry error resulted in the square footage being recorded at 5,200. As a result, the assessment increased from the intended $300,000 to $400,000.

House B was assessed as if it had a finished basement and third floor, as do all of the other houses in House B's development. The assessor calculated the finished square footage to be 5,200. In fact, House B has neither a finished basement nor third floor and its actual finished square footage is 2,500. Had the assessor known that the house did not have this extra finished space, the house's assessment would have dropped from $400,000 to $300,000.

Neither owner appealed the tax valuation in 2010. Both learned of the mistakes made by the tax office in 2011 and asked for a refund of the excess taxes they paid in 2010. How should the Carolina County board of county commissioners respond to these requests?

The Machinery Act permits the tax assessments on both houses to be adjusted for 2011 taxes and future years' taxes. But only the owner of House A is entitled to a refund of 2011 taxes.

The mistake involving House A was a true clerical error because the assessor never intended to assess House A as if it had 5,200 square feet. A refund is justified.

The mistake involving House B did not produce an unintended assessment. Based on the information before the assessor at the time, the assessor intended the assessment for House B to be based on a square footage of 5,200. This was a judgment error, not a clerical error. If the taxpayer disputed this figure, he or she had the obligation to raise the issue during the 2010 appeal process. No refund is justified.

Second, consider clerical errors made by the taxpayer. The Machinery Act permits refunds and releases when taxes are "levied due to clerical error." Because only local governments can levy property taxes, the clerical error in question must be one by a local government and not one by the taxpayer.

A common taxpayer error concerns escrow payments. Many taxpayers escrow their property taxes with their mortgage companies and do not pay those taxes directly. If a taxpayer forgets about the escrow fund and mails a tax payment to the tax office, can that taxpayer get a refund of that payment because the mortgage company will be paying those taxes later in the year? The answer is no, because the payment was for a validly levied tax and the taxpayer's mistake cannot justify a refund. The taxpayer should seek a refund from the mortgage company, not from the tax office.

Another common error arises when a mortgage company sends tax payments for multiple parcels and mistakenly instructs the tax office to apply one of those payments to the wrong parcel. When the mortgage company learns of its mistake, is it entitled to have its payment moved to the correct parcel? Again the answer is no, because moving that tax payment from one parcel to another would constitute a refund of the taxes on the original parcel. Of course, if the tax office made the mistake and applied the payment to the wrong parcel contrary to the mortgage company's instructions, a refund would be justified.

Who Makes the Decision to Authorize a Refund or Release?

The authority to approve refunds and releases lies with the local governing board, not with the tax collector. For small refunds (less than $100), the governing board can delegate the authority to approve refunds and releases to the local government's finance officer, manager, or attorney.

In practice, tax collectors often make routine refunds and seek approval from the board later. For example, if the tax office mistakenly processes a payment for taxes that have already been paid, the tax collector might refund the duplicate payment before seeking permission from the board. Governing boards should discuss this issue with their tax collectors so that all parties are clear on how to proceed before problems arise.

Time Limits on Refunds and Releases

The Machinery Act does not create a time limit for releases of unpaid taxes. But refunds of paid taxes are limited to the later of (1) five years from the date the tax was originally due or (2) six months from the date the taxes were paid (see Table 10).

Table 10. Time Limits on Refunds and Releases under G.S. 105-381

Releases of unpaid taxes	No time limit
Refunds of paid taxes	The later of • 5 years from the original due date *or* • 6 months from the date the taxes were paid

For example, assume that Blue Devil City has been levying taxes on Tommy TarHeel's property for decades under the assumption that Tommy's property is within the city limits. Tommy has paid those taxes each year in a timely fashion. In July of 2012, Tommy has a new survey done that demonstrates that his property is in fact outside the city limits. Tommy immediately asks for a refund of all of the city taxes he's paid since purchasing the property in 1990.

Tommy is clearly entitled to a refund because it is illegal for Blue Devil City to tax property not within its borders. But Tommy's refund is limited by the Machinery Act to those taxes that came due within five years of Tommy's refund request. Taxes on real property are due on September 1 each year. The 2007 taxes were due on September 1, 2007, which is within five years of Tommy's request for a refund. But the 2006 taxes fall outside of that five-year window because they were due on September 1, 2006. And the six-months-from-payment provision does not apply because Tommy paid those taxes back in 2006, long before submitting his refund request. Taxes from years 2005 and earlier similarly fall outside of the refund limitations. As a result, Tommy is entitled to a refund of city taxes only for the years 2007 through 2012.

Questions for Discussion

1. Has your governing board approved any large refunds or releases of property taxes in the past few years? What were the grounds for those approvals?

2. Has your governing board delegated authority to approve refunds of under $100 to the government's manager, attorney, or finance officer?

Registered Motor Vehicles

The taxation of registered motor vehicles (RMVs) is a world unto itself. The rules and practices described in the preceding six chapters do not necessarily apply to taxes levied on RMVs.

To make matters more confusing, in 2005 the General Assembly enacted a law commonly known as House Bill (H.B.) 1779 that will dramatically change the RMV taxation process. Originally intended to take effect in 2009, H.B. 1779 has seen its implementation date postponed several times. The new process is now expected to be in place by July 2013. This chapter describes both the current process and the process that is likely to exist if and when H.B. 1779 is fully implemented.

The Basics

Fortunately, some aspects of RMV taxation will remain the same regardless of when H.B. 1779 takes effect.

Local governments will still levy taxes on RMVs at the same tax rate levied on other types of personal property and on real property. The uniformity provisions in the N.C. Constitution discussed in "The Property Tax Rate," above, prohibit local governments from taxing RMVs at different rates than those applied to other property within their jurisdictions.

RMV taxes will still be triggered by the registration of the motor vehicle with the state Division of Motor Vehicles (DMV). Because registration dates are staggered throughout the year for most motor vehicles, there will still be different property tax years for different RMVs.

The RMV Tax Process until July 2013

Under the existing system, property taxes are levied on motor vehicles *after* they are registered with the DMV. Roughly two months after a registration or renewal, the DMV notifies the appropriate county assessor, who then assigns a tax value to the vehicle and prepares the tax bill. This bill must include all county and city taxes on the RMV, even if the city in question does not rely on the county to collect its regular property taxes.

Taxes on an RMV are due four months after registration or renewal, with interest generally accruing on unpaid taxes one month after the due date. Interest accrues on RMV taxes at a higher rate in the first month than it does for regular property taxes: 5 percent for RMV taxes as compared to 2 percent for regular taxes. However, the additional 3 percent of interest that accrues on RMV taxes must be turned over to the DMV to pay for the development of the new computer software that will implement the new tax system under H.B. 1779. Just as it does for regular property taxes, interest accrues on delinquent RMV taxes at a rate of 0.75 percent per month beginning in the second month of delinquency.

Once unpaid taxes begin to accrue interest, they are considered delinquent and can be subject to enforced collection remedies. Because RMV taxes are not liens on real property, foreclosure is not an option for their collection. But tax collectors may use attachment and garnishment to target the taxpayer's bank accounts and wages or levy and sale to target the taxpayer's personal property. Often the motor vehicle itself is seized and sold by the tax collector to satisfy the taxes it generated.

Four months after the due date—eight months after registration or renewal—the tax collector may ask the DMV to block future renewals of the motor vehicle's registration if the taxes remain unpaid. While the block can be an effective collection remedy, it does not affect the taxpayer until the existing registration expires months later. And many taxpayers will simply avoid renewing their registrations—and risk tickets for driving unregistered vehicles—to avoid having to pay the delinquent property taxes on those vehicles.

Table 11 presents an example of how the current RMV tax system works.

The RMV Tax Process after July 2013

When H.B. 1779 is implemented, vehicle owners will be required to pay the property taxes on their vehicles at the time of registration or renewal. If the taxes are not paid, the owner will not be able to obtain or renew the registration. The new system essentially eliminates the existing lag time between the registration of a vehicle and the billing and collection of property taxes on that vehicle.

Table 11. RMV Taxes under the Existing System

Assume that Tommy TarHeel registers his new Chevy pick-up truck in November 2012.	
Registration date	November 12, 2012
Ownership, situs, and taxability determined	November 12, 2012
Tax value determined as of	January 1, 2013
RMV tax year	December 2012–December 2013
Tax rate	Rate in effect for the 2012–2013 fiscal year
Due date	March 1, 2013
Interest begins	April 1, 2013
Tax collector may ask DMV to block renewal	July 2014

Responsibility for assigning tax values and collecting the taxes will shift from counties to the state. The N.C. Department of Revenue will develop statewide schedules of tax values for motor vehicles, with adjustments for local market conditions. The DMV will collect both registration fees and local property taxes at the time of registration or renewal, with the latter passed along to the appropriate local governments minus a small collection fee retained by the state.

The new system will provide exceptions for automobile dealers, where buyers will be able to obtain two-month registrations on new vehicles without paying the property taxes on those vehicles. After the new owners pay the taxes, the temporary registrations will become valid for the entire tax year.

In a nutshell, the new system should eventually reduce the administrative burden on counties for RMV taxes and should improve collection rates. Taxpayers may benefit from the consolidation of the registration and taxation transactions. That said, the transition will require substantial training and education for state and local officials as well as for the millions of taxpayers who will be navigating the new system.

Other Local Taxes on Motor Vehicles

In addition to property taxes, both counties and cities have the authority to generate other revenues from motor vehicles.

In 2009 the General Assembly granted counties the authority to levy a registration tax of up to $7 per year that is collected by the DMV at the time of registration. However, this tax is permitted only if the county or one of the local governments in the county operates a public transportation system. And the proceeds from this tax may be used only for the creation or operation of that public transportation system.

All municipalities are authorized to levy taxes on the privilege of operating a motor vehicle within their borders of up to $5 per vehicle, plus an additional $5 per vehicle if the municipality operates a public transportation system. The General Assembly has granted a number of municipalities the authority to levy additional motor vehicle privilege taxes of up to $30 per vehicle. These taxes are generally collected by the county along with property taxes on the vehicle. After H.B. 1779 takes effect, the DMV will be responsible for collecting these taxes at the time of registration.

Questions for Discussion

1. What was your local government's total tax levy on RMVs last year?

2. What was your local government's collection rate for RMV taxes last year? How did that compare to its collection rate for regular property taxes?

3. Does your county levy a registration tax on RMVs? Does your municipality levy a privilege license tax on RMVs? If so, how much are those taxes per vehicle?

Appendix: Additional Resources

Denning, Shea Riggsbee. *A Guide to the Listing, Assessment, and Taxation of Property in North Carolina.* Chapel Hill, NC: UNC School of Government, 2009.

McLaughlin, Christopher B. *Fundamentals of Property Tax Collection Law in North Carolina.* Chapel Hill, NC: UNC School of Government, 2012.

Millonzi, Kara A. *Local Government Revenue Sources in North Carolina.* Chapel Hill, NC: UNC School of Government, 2011.